Beasts

Krišjānis Zeļģis

About the translator

Jayde Will is a literary translator working from Lithuanian, Latvian, and Estonian. His recent or forthcoming translations include Daina Tabūna's short story collection *The Secret Box* (The Emma Press), Ričardas Gavelis's novel *Memoirs of a Life Cut Short* (Vagabond Voices), Artis Ostups's poetry collection *Gestures* (Ugly Duckling Presse), and Inga Pizāne's poetry collection *Having Never Met* (A Midsummer Night's Press). He lives in Riga.

Beasts

Krišjānis Zeļģis

Translated from Latvian by Jayde Will

PARTHIAN

Supported by the Ministry of Culture for the Republic of
Latvia and the Latvian Writers' Union

Kultūras ministrija

Latvijas Rakstnieku savienība   Latvija 100

CYNGOR LLYFRAU CYMRU
WELSH BOOKS COUNCIL

Parthian, Cardigan SA43 1ED
www.parthianbooks.com
First published in 2018
ISBN 9781912109074
Design and layout by Alison Evans
Printed by Pulsio

contents

the professionals

secrets

beasts

❌❖❌

I don't know what's depicted there
but it gives me a lot of strength
to think ahead
imagine
that I assemble everything together
like an all-encompassing theory
you shouldn't think in line segments
there is no real beginning
no real end
a flooded watercolour
in which for reasons known only to me
you muddy the waters
to me what's important is free time and doing nothing
free time and doing nothing are important to me

✖✖✖

the beasts are eating
the atmospheric pressure gently caresses their fur
behind the fence where we stand – perspective
always perspective
all those things distant and foreign
let's talk about how we're doing
is it love
say it
say it

my brother is leaning on a chest of drawers
he is staring intently into the distance
lost in thought
in the autumn he returned from the army and asked
me to make pancakes for him
even if they're made out of rye flour
in the summer he drowned
while swimming across the lake

isn't that a clever little bird
that makes nests in countless big trees
isn't that an evil wicked bird
whose song makes me remember

a platform in the forest
where you can shoot at gullible animals
that come to eat for free
all sorts of eyes in the dark you can see how they shine
but we didn't come here to shoot just watch
the beasts don't know that and rattle the box
come down here they shout
and threaten to break our skulls
with hardened rye bread
I am afraid
but I understand that it's a beauty
that can't be acquired easily

in the night a dog came and sat next to us
in the night
on the steppe
when there's nothing
except darkness
stretching and running in its vastness
not catching on anything
just our hair
that has coarsened
from the cold water

I waited for the whale
for a few days before I ate various kinds
of seafood
I sharpened my dagger I kind of knew I would just watch
the unfamiliar acquaintances gathered
in thick canvas coats
they fight with the wind and look right where I am
the field of vision like a field of battle
I hide and don't reveal my gaze
I want to be the one who shouts
hey look there's a whale
pointing in the right direction with my finger
I know that everyone else also silently hopes
for that brief moment of glory
the grey dirty sea rocks
and no whales appear at all
it doesn't really mean anything
it can happen
it could also happen tomorrow
today it didn't tomorrow it will

I can't drink
I am too young
like an ingrown birch tree
and I understand how it is when you wreck a wedding banquet
your life's biggest feast

foxes who have been run over would nod in agreement

he puts his clothes on
as the police arrive
and take away his gas pistol
he can't find his shoes
and he has to take someone else's slippers
the landlord
angrily pursued him in his wellies
I can't understand how that happens
a normal day changes
the landlord shouts strange words
until there's no pursuer in the English park anymore
just squirrels still hoping for a practical joke

it turns out the fields begin already at the end of the street
I drive along the golden avenue
leaves stick to wet tyres
it's not clear how long that could last
I want to get to the point
which an unknown person had marked
as the last thing that is worth seeing
there wasn't anything there
a clearing with ditches
where rabbits are stranded

a bittern a chiffchaff and a common dunlin
gorge on smorgasbord leftovers from my bag
two slices of white bread and also two
cherry plums of a yellow colour
it can't be
but the birds' songs confirm it
today an afternoon snack will be skipped
a greedy little stomach small as a
clenched fist
grumbles angry at the World Wildlife Fund
member in fieldwork conditions

I counted the dead while looking out the window
out of horror
out of boredom to find out what's left
the shops' empty mouths and happy dogs
that don't suspect a thing
there's already scratching at the door
together with the water it floods into my system
in my day there's a point where I can stop
but I have to save up for something bigger
always barely getting by
the best always ahead of you

while I was asleep at the wheel
and hit a deer
you were all sitting in the
back reeling off jokes
and telling stories of the comical
misunderstandings during your trips
it seemed like a dream until your brother
called me and said that I'd have to pay for
the paint job
light cheerful music was playing
as if nothing was going to happen
and now a beautiful brown creature will never
crunch sweet spring sprouts anymore

oh what a feast we had
with venison olives marinated steaks and classic
delicious cutlets in different sauces
and potatoes with the hidden happiness inside flooded
    the guests' faces
if I were a deer I'd be delighted in
this surprisingly practical approach to death

a grey-haired man's song
while swinging a dog lead
where is it

someone is transporting trees
through the park
for cutting
dead giants
with roots in past centuries
in the end the dog appears
it gazes at what the calloused hand is hiding
a treat

✕◇✕

I fell asleep near the lake on her towel
the smell of washing from her shirt
while she swims
everything is peaceful and quiet
other than that nothing's new
I talk with people and
in the mornings I dig up small animal bones

you smell of pine

＊＊＊

between the cinnamon and the coffee you're standing
with childhood's lips
just as beautiful as I remember
through the curtains
and blankets drying outside
time is as long as a telephone number

✕✕✕

you smell of pine
of a trunk in the forest around which a beach breeze is sneaking
your hair tangled in the branch's fingers
my tongue tangled coaxing your ears
so you would follow
I do that
I'm like that

industrial legacy

a strong bass is present in everything you do
you dress in the kitchen because of the light
the warmth remains on your flesh like a mark
which came along from the sheets
the city has switched on all its chimneys and waits
you already feel the industrial revolution at your door
an entire century in your hallway

I'm at home but there's no electricity
the fridge melts quietly in the dark
magnets obligingly hold on to
an unreadable message
I am cold
buy some soup
love

the morning chill gets up with us
when we look for the road out of the forest
it hugs us without saying goodbye
still it comes along with moss and the smell of deer
the sleeping bags' dampness presses up to our thighs
goose bumps come and go like the longing for
shop snacks and normal food
we go towards the roar towards the motorway's artery
where we will be happily suckling
our legs knock against the stumps where we stood yesterday
looking for a place to sleep
you get up on a stump and look at me so grandly

needle

you sit in front of the fireplace
sunk in the chair so your feet don't get cold
you sit and work around the bone
using a flint
you slowly fashion a needle out of cattle bone
a needle with which you can sew together pieces of leather
for your next project
your forehead wrinkled like you're angry
your fingers cramped beautifully
your lips moving
shoo shoo shoo

the basis of our relationship is a table
parameters filled in neat columns
which reflect a piece of a personality
a table is what you turn to
if the course is unclear
or some triviality has crept in

still a table is just a table
it doesn't whisper what's right
it doesn't give you a hint
what to do with your life
tormented by stress and uncertainty
I look at it and quietly beg
for the answer to come on its own

something has to happen
you can feel it when I wake up you hug me like a bear cub
your strong arms are your business card
a drowsy awakening drips from the teapot spout
if someone comes to the door
tell them I'm gone
I took my coat without saying goodbye
maybe you even cry on purpose then
he didn't return

the café where you work on the corner of the big junction
a piece of railroad workers' cake
before work
as if I didn't know
take along some sandwiches
coffee
me

we were heading to the station Belorusskaya
the metro's wind stirs the heavy air
breakfast behind us
with a dry meat pie and over-sweet tea
it was clear from the beginning
that you could expect only mutual evil here
she won't stop crying even
as the cops check our passports
and take a bribe
it's Belorusskaya I tell her
there's no place to retreat there's just a wall
a dirty cigarette-smeared wall

against me

When a strong wind is blowing it feels
like everything is against me

A. Krivade

I have no money
a bill at a Japanese restaurant for maki sushi
with cucumber and avocado and jasmine green tea
why do I always get stuck with the bill
while you piss and powder your nose
or talk on the phone with your sister
the conversations are about the theatre and your famous friends
who you smoke weed with and fuck
we plan to meet up again and be more open next time
it's a long walk home
it's cold
I'm afraid to get on the tram without a ticket
I say it's fine
for a week I eat oats potatoes and the neighbours' sausage I stole
along with the new year come new meetings
and in my wallet there are fish scales for prosperity

kids like that don't sleep long in the morning
they crawl to the light through the pillows
in winter there's just a few hours of the right hue
artificial light ruins everything on the canvas like poison
the children have to paint quickly while there's snow

I didn't want him to start talking
about horoscopes Kali Yuga
homeopathy and reiki
but he started precisely with that
without giving me the slightest chance to settle in to the surprise
of an Australian roaming around this corner of the world
I quietly hoped that he would turn all this into a joke
make those lame conspiracies disappear
still he didn't stop
with every word distancing himself
from an offer to stay at my place or invitation for a drink
even his name didn't seem to be important anymore
maybe it was Kevin
who remembers the names of strangers picked up in a car
still for a moment
before everything was ruined
for 10 km at the beginning of the journey
he seemed to be the best person I had
met that day

I'm not giving you my shirt
the world is far too complicated
for you to understand
that ships have sunk transporting the wool home

time has stopped and it isn't love
the doctor is fiddling about
while looking for the patient's file
then I say my ID number from memory
numerous times
the state-heated walls are tone deaf
I gesture helplessly while waiting
to get the ink back
in my fingertips
however they will wait for me outside
an entire queue of big and angry yokels
nailing me to the wall with their eyes
while the doctor is sitting in safety
I don't feel so ill anymore
after all the tests I don't feel
ill at all

your *fuck you* in your text message
and a migraine for the second day in a row
are my most recent heaps of clouds
my *cumulonimbus*
perhaps someone put a curse on you
grandma bugs me
maybe it really is a curse
if you always do what you want
then why am I unhappy

everything smells like urine
good that I woke up
a nineteen-year-old girl stole my shoes on
the train
the factory hasn't paid wages for months already
I caught her at the end of the carriage and struck her
it's the second winter my mum's house isn't heated
no one is paying any attention that I have socks with holes
   in them
bitch I think to myself
the bank isn't answering the phone anymore
I put on my only shoes and shake myself
she is standing with her head bent down
and blood from her nose drips on her skirt
sorry I say
the dead don't have coffins
and they would be the last that would deserve
a bite of our lives
while returning I see that my bag had been nicked
mackerel tins eight of them
no one saw anything
no one
saw a thing

after uni you will go back to your hometown
where you'll be alone once again
the only people you know in this town
are the racist idiots from your secondary school years
and your parents

the rest of the people
the ones you love
the ones you miss
live abroad now
or died
or betrayed you

you lie saying that you're a cheery person
sadness suits you much better
there's no one near that could hug you
this stupid Internet between us
I look speechlessly into your brown eyes of despair
and I do nothing

I had to travel for two full weeks
freeze in sleeping cars for many nights in a row
dead tired I chat with myself about nothing
running from all that cold once again
I have reached the empty frost-covered yard
just this time it is a much quieter situation
I sit on a mattress and slowly chew
half a yellow paracetamol

dear Anna
we can't reach you
we can't hear your voice
we're concerned
French music is playing but it's not helping
a kind of dizziness from worry inside when you don't know
are you in your motherland or in some smelly airport
waiting to be picked up
like children who are picked up from nursery by their parents
we would come drive and hurry
but we don't know where you are
we think a lot about you
but I doubt that helps when you're cold
and you're tired of terrible fast food

pick up the phone
please
we want to take care of you

evil

if he is tired or ill
melancholic
or content
but his sleep and appetite dwindle
for a very brief moment he becomes a better person
and with that I think
less dangerous

*

his strength can only take the shape of words
and it's wrong to assume that they will have preserved
their original clearly defined meaning
he will either become a prophet or continue to feed his fear
in both cases
becoming weaker day by day

*

he doesn't pretend he's going back in time
and correcting long acknowledged mistakes
it's more like working past the borders
of disappearing and forgetting
and that suits me

✖✖✖

who even talks like that
who speaks like that with an older person
wait for him to address you
extend your hand
squeeze it tight
but not too tight
not briefly
but also not agonisingly long
wait he will definitely address you

I'm really cold
it's probably from sleeping
on the damp shore of the river
death cuts me slice by slice in my sleep
upon waking I am quieter than usual
like I've shrunk into myself
I should probably look for a job
something respectable that suits a man my age

the professionals

four humid summers

it was in Vancouver
where I designed
my first
full-scale classic Chinese garden
an entire bus park had to be demolished
a metal forest with rusty tops
reddish brown tops
when the park was carved up
placed in massive shipping containers
and taken out of the city
I felt better
now I couldn't say
that on some level I didn't care anymore

×○×

I would like my children to see what I do
so they could come down with me
deep into the mineshaft
hear how the water drips in damp passages
marvel at how the tunnels are made
how they meet at right angles
the precise amount of explosives
in order to make this brutal beauty
which is my every day
the sum of my skills and education

some of us try to talk about it
but we just stare at the TV camera speechless
unable to show more than a twilit
empty silence

the priest

once again asleep I see an answer in a dream
quietly caressing the edge of the sheet I get up
leaving my notes untouched

it's just the paper I don't like
I sleep in the foyer waiting for mass
I don't want to speak
which is why words that come from the flesh seem much
   more mine

the white days of emptiness which burn your eyes when
   you look
an endlessness that swallows up all your efforts
in whose name am I waking up at night
as if I remember as if I knew

He will pick me up I cannot drive
I slip my finger into the boiling beef stock

the garnish should be cut in
3 mm thick slices
I'm afraid that work is sucking me dry

chicory and fresh courgette flowers
we will meet in the backyard after work

blanch the tomatoes and press the garlic
he'll be waiting in the car

take the asparagus by the ends and peel it
I'm waiting
the leeks are degorging for seven minutes

you're here
make a marinade from cream vinegar mustard horse radish
salt and pepper
I hide my finger
quietly scraping the car window I ask you to let me in

before serving - wash
dry and cut it into fine rings
you talk about your day

I don't have anything to tell you

how to describe it
driving through Lviv in a tourist bus
the trap of history has tragically snapped shut
the guide leaning on her elbows
for years yawningly telling
the same thing over and over

the cartographer

in blue striped pyjama bottoms
you go to your work desk and draw beautiful maps
you invent yet another projection of the world
when your eyes become red you go out and smoke
you inhale long lazy wisps in a defined rhythm
your life repeats itself so clearly that I could draw it
all down
table
door
ashtray

I work in the Romanian embassy
And in the morning in packets of mayonnaise
I carry the sun with me
the winters are so hard here in the North
the sadness of consular duties
an office romance
how can you simply get through your days
with wet straw legs
I wade my way towards you mayonnaise packet
you will be the death of my eggs for breakfast

the printing house has its own events
the colour eats into your hair and fingers black from work
speed and precision
are my mastered instincts

the air smells of intellect
of new books
of a steaming pot of coffee that is cooling down
my shift seems like one brief smoke break

at night I think to myself
I don't even want a holiday
I say to my wife
I am a professional and
letting the letters *f* and *i* collide is careless

the lights went out in the hall
a fuse had blown
from the long wait the electrician had passed out
in his chamber of misery
spilling the beer all over the panel board
without even waking up
when the manager walked in
she had little bits of foam
at the corners of her mouth

secrets

I started my walk with Huseyin who is in the vegetable drying business.

T. Satana

there will be fruit juice for breakfast
I stayed awake on purpose
in the night I thought
right when the shop opens
I will be right there even planned out what to say
I am waiting with bleary eyes
when the flat will wake up
I will be *nonchalant* and you too
will *nonchalantly* suck down the juice
with yesterday's straws
while talking about some jam-packed
plans for the day

but I can still sleep for another
fifteen minutes or so
however after that
who knows who knows

there were four days I don't remember
clearly at all
strangers called me by my first name and incorrect last name
I learned to drink all over again
as if broken I glided on the weary river
the leaves fell and those asleep in the boats
slowly forgot everything

greeting rituals

with a name you can never remember
the first few times
never knowing for sure which one to address you with
you can suddenly leave on a train
without waiting for a fried flounder and relatives
still during the first half of the day
you were getting a tan and everything seems fine
how all this is holding together I don't know

such a wide crossing with a beeping sound for the blind
that even someone with sight can't cross it in time
I see
in a Polish bus driving past
a schoolgirl giving me the finger

Antwerpen port

I searched wading through the swampy fields
where the muddy ditches voraciously sloshed up to my
    boot tips
from the effort my beating heart balled into a fist
that same street and time
you the embankment's concrete mouth are already smiling
but I move like a point on a navigation map
a small nimble pointer which traipses forward
at its strange speed
the freight is lowered into the deep mouths of the ships
my drying throat so ineptly weak

a plummeting plane which loses a wing
the field where it will soon crash hasn't been harvested yet
an entire village will be left without crops
because the rescuers the ambulance
the police the army and the curious crowd
will trample everything that hasn't been burned

beyond the hill you can already hear
the sirens of the firefighters
the last day of summer slowly passes

I accidentally got off the train to Minsk
a guy was sitting in the window in front of me
it seemed this person was like
a brother who had fallen in the war
just in different clothes
hidden behind the curtain he was quietly reading
Russian newspapers
I wrote my phone number on a piece of paper
but he just smiled strangely
secrets

the bamboo plants brought outside for summer
next to which you drink coke and wait
from under the nose of the cashier you steal
those small utterly worthless trinkets
you take this joy as a discount
the northerly pale light
where it is always a little bit cold

Roman holiday

a warm light that rises up in each shot
you sit and show off your sandals
thin leather strips are highlighting the curve of your feet
you sit ever so simply
with an expression you can't find in books
or on the Internet
or in a secret mailing list
knowledge as power is hiding in the architecture
all around you

there isn't any time here
and as you hold the pine nuts
while I shell them
sorry I spit them out
behind your back
a bonfire with tea and Russian archaeologists
who are so wrapped up in their conversation
that you can only look
with a gaping mouth
there isn't any time here
the steppe has already been looking through us in the
  emptiness for a week

in '88 my life turned upside down
I understood I don't believe in anything anymore
I went to talk with the village priest
while walking along the lake I said
don't be upset Pāvels
I did everything I possibly could

To the west Time Killers! (A. Akmentina)

like vegetables that have travelled more than us
we also rot in the countryside
you have to roll back the tape before you return it
if you know what tape is
children don't know what roll film is anymore
and they are six years old

with scrupulous precision the cold
breaks the fine birch branches
the day after tomorrow at the latest
everything will be over and out of happiness
we will dive into the park's cool bars hastily constructed
out of leftover lumber
which smells of resin
and fresh air
the ozone itself will descend
into our lungs
with all of its concrete
and salt mixture
it's such a long and agonising winter
but slowly the snow and ice accumulates
the waters of March

I stop the car
and listen to
my passenger pissing outside
with his face facing a mowed eternity
flat and stingy Zemgale
empty as a plate licked clean

I'm afraid I don't know these people
why are you showing me these photos
I sat here totally by chance waiting until it starts
it could have been any other person and you
would also say
that is my graduating class
that young man on the right edge is me

Parthian Baltic Poetry

The Moon is a Pill

Aušra Kaziliūnaitė

Phenomena

Eduards Aivars

The Rules of Bird Hunting

Eeva Park

Narcoses

Madara Gruntmane

New Baltic Poetry

Edited by Jayde Will

Now I Understand

Marius Burokas

PARTHIAN

www.parthianbooks.com